The Secret Road:
Walking with Persephone

poems by

Barbara Segal

Finishing Line Press
Georgetown, Kentucky

The whole world is a single flower.
—*Zen Master Seun Sahn*

The Secret Road:
Walking with Persephone

Copyright © 2021 by Barbara Segal
ISBN 978-1-64662-717-2 First Edition
All rights reserved under International and Pan-American Copyright Conventions. No part of this book may be reproduced in any manner whatsoever without written permission from the publisher, except in the case of brief quotations embodied in critical articles and reviews.

ACKNOWLEDGMENTS

I thank the following journals for their publication of these individual poems in previous versions:

Oberon ~ "In the Village of Love and Loss"
PPA Literary Review ~ "A Rescue" (excerpted from the longer, prize-winning poem, "Pawley's Island, South Carolina")
The Avocet ~ "Cooling earth and skies;" "October sunset;" "Warm days, cool nights"
2021 Haiku Calendar ~ "White dogwoods"
The Long Island Quarterly, 25th Anniversary Issue ~ "Where water is land and land, water"
Bard's Annual 2020 ~ "This Summer Night"
"Crossing Over" is forthcoming as "Vigil" in the anthology *Paumanok, Transition* (Island Sound Press)

Publisher: Leah Huete de Maines
Editor: Christen Kincaid
Cover Art: Barbara Segal
Author Photo: Vincent Gattorno
Cover Design: Elizabeth Maines McCleavy

Order online: www.finishinglinepress.com
also available on amazon.com

Author inquiries and mail orders:
Finishing Line Press
PO Box 1626
Georgetown, Kentucky 40324
USA

Table of Contents

The Electric Universe 1
An Object in Motion, Wanting Stillness.. 2
The Secret Road 3
The White Narcissus 4
Abduction 5
Persephone's Letter Home 6
She Begins to See 7
She Emerges 8
Enchantment 9
Surrounded by ghosts 10
She Wants His Name 11
Where land is water, and water, land 12
Meditation Circling Time and Space 13
A Rescue 14
This Summer Night 15
My dearest Hades 16
Persephone the Older and Wiser.. 18
On the Cusp of November 19
The Moon Balances at the Apex 20
Hearing the Winter Night 21
Winter Dream 23
Of Darkness and Light 24
In the Village of Love and Loss 26
Our Sacred Path 28
Crossing Over 29
Quiet, Not Always Peaceful 30
Her Dystopian Vision 31
Even a Goddess Despairs 32
A Dialectic Tale for Our Time 33
Temple of the Goddess 34
Persephone did not come with me to Florida 35
Special Acknowledgments 36

The Electric Universe
> *a resonating dream of the electric universe* —William Kentridge

1.

Orbs of red and orange light glow,
pass steadily through stems and leaves
of the houseplant on my windowsill.
Photosynthesis right before my eyes.

2.

My second child is born safe,
but I am in mortal danger,
am wheeled off, put under,
witness the whole universe
interconnected,
a cosmic light board,
red, yellow, blue, green,
blinking on, blinking off,
a relay of colors
passing energy
from one to the next:
a *dream of the electric universe.*

3.

Brushing translucent hues on paper,
each colored shape blooms
in dialogue with its neighbors—
small universes.

An Object in Motion, Wanting Stillness

I drive the gray expressway east in Friday traffic, flying with clipped wings,
   rumbling speed bumps pulling me back on track when I begin to wander.
Migraine marches across my head, the road, the journey.

Finally, a two-lane country road—farms holding the land, trees holding the sky,
   vineyards, farm stands, small towns,
honest brown ground, furrowed, reaching out, holding me.

At a friend's Jamesport cottage, camaraderie of four women sharing tea
   and sweets, a fine doo-wop concert and dinner in town, ice cream,
a sleepover on strawberry-pink sheets.

I wake with a dragon-red eye, a burst blood vessel, souvenir of megrim,
   and a strong urge to return home.

Around the corner,
>   alone in morning fog
>   dark shape of fisherman
>   on sandy shore

Swift as an osprey on a thermal, morning breeze blows me home through a soft,
   yellow-infused world,
>   stacked in circling layers
>   in the awakening sky,
>   five turkey vultures

Next day, pulling weeds, pruning plant and bush, making order and space in
   garden and mind,
I dead-head iris, set stakes for morning glories to twine, remove purple purslane,
   creeping Charlie, henbit,
>   at the pond
>   below Japanese maples
>   koi surface

The Secret Road

Alone in a desert of sparse wildflowers,
frightened, lost, seeking answers for my being,

I sit on the ground, take out pencils and paper,
draw the flowers to life upon a page.

They dance, they curtsy, flirt, speak.
A revelation, for I had not known the gift inside,

the artist who can transform simple things
with paint or words, and create objects of beauty.

In that moment I reach for the beauty, a flower,
as Persephone once did.

The White Narcissus

Sun warms her back, motes glimmer
in golden air. Bees laze from flower to flower,
buzz and hum across the broad garden of meadow.

She reaches for a dazzling white narcissus—
and the earth rips open with a thunderous crack,
electrifies her hair, sucks all breath from her body.

Abduction

Red-eyed, pawing the air,
foam flying from their mouths,
four raven-black horses burst from below
pulling a black and gold chariot.

An arm snakes out, grabs her,
pulls her inside. The horses wheel,
hurtle back down the long tunnel of death
that steals all sweet sound and light.

In the bleakness of the underworld
a deep voice professes love and desire,
says she is to be his queen,
seats her on a black marble throne.

She cries without cease for her mother,
her friends, her fields of flowers and light.
In this dismal land there are no blooms,
only withering willows along the river of oblivion,

and a small pomegranate tree with red fruits.
The gardener offers their seeds to her,
but she cannot eat, cannot be consoled,
wants only her mother.

Persephone's Letter Home

Dear Mother,

All dark as crows on a moonless night,
black, bleak, a void of loneliness.
I was crying, crying, empty as death,
bereft, dearest Mother, without you.
Time stilled, and eventually I felt safer,
my tears ceased, fears released
like paper boats on a river.

Mother, strong as any friend's, I feel
his love for me. Here in Hades flowers
wither. *I*, though, blossom and grow.
I find joy in being cherished as the rarest
rose. His kindness and tenderness teach me
love deep as my heart, deep as the Ionian Sea.

Life here is nigh to night, quiet, ordered,
somber. I work alongside Hades, help
the troubled, unsettled ones find
their final place of rest and peace.

Today my soul sings—soon I will return to you,
not as the child taken from you, but as a woman
of her own mind and stature, of desires I freely
profess to relish, and of purpose I embrace.

With jubilance, I anticipate our reunion.

Your daughter,
Persephone

She Begins to See

She is opening her eyes,
shivering, shaking,

is learning
flowers do not bloom in darkness,

sunshine and sweetness
are only part of life's equation;

a father can sell you out
to abduction and rape,

even one as powerful as Zeus,
king of gods.

She emerges

keen as a robin listening for the worm,
smells earth rising fresh from snowmelt
readying to receive roots, bulbs, seeds.

Eager to leave behind winter's punishments,
she longs to embrace spring,
to shed heavy garments with sun's increase.

Birds return, chorus their joy,
lift her with their lilting music,
new songs ringing every day.

Snowdrops and crocus color her gray garden,
green growing shoots and stems promise
tulip, daffodil, hyacinth, iris,

the swelling red buds of maple,
yellow of forsythia,
marvel of a blooming plum.

She is reborn.

Enchantment

He lands like an angel,
wings back-stretched, iridescent,
then in a blink transmutes into a robin.

The shaman's at work again she thinks,
moving past a mass of Siberian iris,
deep red buds on blue-green stalks,
a few blooms perched like purple birds.

Ruffled by a mild breeze, lemon columbines
flutter, ferns unfurl their spirals, spiders weave
sticky webs of words and symbols.

Water splashes, drops from rock to rock into the pond.
Koi of all colors swim slowly within.
Persephone revels in spring's pleasures.

Surrounded by ghosts,

she mourns, a phalanx of wildflowers around her,
thin protection from piercing pain.

Aura of fear and sadness encircles her, memories haunt:
near-born children could never bloom in Hades' darkness.

Tiny, hungry ghosts dangle before her;
soul wounds never heal.

Today she is a butterfly blown
against hawthorn's sharp branches.

She Wants His Name

A fracas of sound above.

She wants his name.

Name that blots out light
like dark ink spilled across a page.

He cuts black shapes
into innocent blue skies,

overshadows paltry smiles,
empty conversation.

Smell of dark musk,
blackness flaring blue.

Eyes gleam bottomless depths,
see into the void.

He speaks in hoarse tones,
flaps warnings,
flies in high circles,
aims arrow-straight,
dawdles, taunts.

Crow knows.

She wants his name.

Where land is water, and water, land,

lightning twists across cloud-dark sky in a shock of silver filament.
The gray-misted marsh is muted by rain's flailing curtain. Last thunder
rumbles off, raindrops slow. Shore color returns with emerging sun—
lime, sienna, mahogany, darker tones at the tree line across the roiling river.
A lone white egret dazzles.

Meditation Circling Time and Space

Murmuration of birds
kaleidoscope of sky
air and clouds vast to horizon
land and water interweaving
sun and rain exchanging
cycling the wheel of water and salt
of eddies ripples waves and tides
time turning in arcs and orbs
of earth moon sun and stars
spinning revolving ever changing
tumbling moving rearranging

A Rescue

Along the surf line
a small jellyfish,
stubby hydrant
of translucence,
parasol rimmed
in maroon,
pulsates light
within,
still alive.
I scoop it up,
throw it back
to the sea.

This Summer Night

Katydids knit the distance
between *a* and *b*,
first chorus and second,
nearer and farther.

Their sounds and rhythms
stitch together
a neighbor's trees
with mine.

My old Japanese maple
unfolds its umbrella of stars
over the pond
of slow-dreaming koi.

This summer night
I rise from bed,
pen these words,
think of you.

My dearest Hades,

I send you nine sunset messages of the wheel:

        March, 5:40 pm

Like a Hokusai—
white clouds and blue sky,
shy pink blushes.

        April, 7:30 pm

Tulips hold last drops
in their cups, sunset reflections.
Drink in now .

        May, 8:30 pm

White dogwoods
disappearing into dusk,
gone.

        June, 8:45 pm

Roses sigh with perfume,
dream of mist.
I breathe in deeply.

        July, 8:30 pm

Black clouds tower,
lightning bolts sizzle, strike.
Rain rushes down.

        August, 7:40 pm

Scarlet sails glide
across ruby sky:
sailors delight.

September, 7 pm

Warm days, cool nights—
crickets and locusts serenade
in rhythmic rounds.

October, 6:30 pm

Red leaves challenge
as sun salvos fire.
Leaves fall in surrender.

November, 4:50 pm

Cooling earth and skies,
geese migrate, swallows, hawks—
winter's door opens.

Soon I return to you, dearest.

My love eternally,
Persephone

Persephone the Older & Wiser

Sees the full Flower Moon
    glide across a lilac sky.
Welcomes the lunar pull on her pulse.

Hears forest trees
    scissor the wind.
Draws cards—the High Priestess.

Wears a vestment of down & deer hide,
    feathers & beads in her long hair.
Raises her arms in grateful supplication.

Removes gleaming ruby pomegranate seeds
    from lacy maze of membrane,
eats, lets the juices run.

Gathers treasures of feathers, pods, branches
    & bone,
arranges them in sacred messages.

Ignores ambient voices
    for the quiet one within.
No longer needs his attentions, only his respect.

Journeys in the arc of season,
    the circle of time.

On the Cusp of November

I feel the earth turning
away from the sun, moving on
in longer shadows, darker skies.

Leaves lose their vital green,
let go one by one, tumble
to the frosty ground.

Mallards huddle at the harbor,
fly out by day, migrate
to southern light.

I observe my flowers seed
and die back; harvest squash,
tomatoes; pick apples and pears.

I, too, will soon release,
retreat, shelter within
until sun's return.

The Moon Balances at the Apex

I stand below the night trees,
feel the moon's unblinking gaze
right to my soul, welcome

its luminous, penetrating mystery,
watch the orb align, curve slowly away—
radiance moving through dark skies.

My inward eye turns to the pond.
I see the koi below the ice, frozen—
a mobile of shapes and colors, waiting.

They will sense when to leave stasis,
will return to movement when cold yields
to spring's rooting and warmth.

Like the fish and moon, I will know.

hearing the winter night

wind
is knocking
banging

on the door
and windows

cold vast night
holds the noise

and stars

points of light
prick the dark

stars so far
I can't hear them

but I know
their song

sky so high
and quiet

half-moon
a glowing bowl

no milk
in it

demi-lune
of moon

no bluster

high
above waving branches

high

sky

full

of moon
and wind
and stars

Winter Dream

My naked branches reach high into icy skies, seeking
light and warmth of sun. At finely branching fingertips,
moss, twigs, grasses, scraps of paper and string weave
a delicate bowl, a sheltering nest for chattering winter birds.
Squirrels and raccoons sleep each night in my hollows and burls.
By my feet, leaves layer a home for beetles, millipedes, spiders.
Clouds pillow my head, my hair, my thoughts and worldly cares.
Torso clothed in bark, I root down deep into the earth.

Of Darkness and Light

1. Darkness

Like dark ink spilled across a page
the earth gapes open,
electrifies my hair, sucks all breath
from my body.

A void of loneliness
dark as crows on a moonless night,
red-eyed, claws the air.

An arm snakes out
moving on in longer shadows,
smell of dark musk.

All black, bleak,
eyes gleaming bottomless depths.
Shards of moonlight splinter the floor.

Her inward eye turns
shivering, shaking,
but beginning to see.

Help me from parched lips,
tiny, hungry ghosts dangle before her.

Crabbed hands reach,
grab at something invisible.
Bedcovers swim oddly.

The ocean, silent,
lies still as death.

2. Light

Bathing in moonlight, soaking in its glowing mystery,
a sea of reeds reach up.
Motes glimmer on gentle air,
kissed and caressed by season and time.

A lantern moving through dark heavens,
a tent of silver sound around her,
she lands like an angel,

gathers treasures of feathers, pods,
branches and bone,
arranges them in sacred messages.

Moon and stars sail
across sweep of night sky,
time turning in arcs and orbs.

A cento of lines selected from the poet's Persephone poems.

In the Village of Love and Loss

       1

I want to keep your memory
imprisoned within a hut
of green silk and sinew,
safe but inaccessible.

My heart is too frail to hold
this harsh sorrow any longer.

Yet, yesterday's frozen snows
are melting, dripping, pouring.

       2

Your heart was damaged, bled long,
long before you gave me life,
bled and dripped into caverns
so deep they were unseen.

Today I bury the harm
as a placenta after birth,
keep you within this earthen
red hut of memory.

       3

You my mirror
lie apart in darkness.

How then
will I see?

4

Your passing so swift,
a light blown out
in chill winds of ice
and snow fallen thick
as prison walls.

5

Our dog howls, paces
the rooms we shared,
is unsettled, disquiet.

Is that you there, sitting
in your corner chair
along the dark wall?

6

Our friends grieve.
I comfort them.

My life continues yours.
Your life continues mine.

Our hut is a temple
of white light.

Our Sacred Path

We walk the hushed white halls,
past doors closed and open.
Within each room, a bed holds
someone in their last days.

We enter, speak gently, take the hand
of the restless woman who is more bird
and air than matter. We lovingly touch
her forehead, shoulder, see her calm.

Next door, a man's breathing is labored,
his eyes are closed. Family is gathered
around him. His wife reverently shows us
a photograph from healthier days,

asks to speak to us of her sorrows—
her young children will be left
fatherless, the crushing stress,
sadness of life without her beloved.

Down the hall a husband flutes folk melodies
for his dying wife, family clapping lightly in time.
From another room an old man moans softly,
wears a clean hospital gown, and the smell
of death.

Together we minister to the dying,
honor the sacredness of life and death.

Crossing Over

Her body moves by breath alone
slowly rising and falling
as a gently rocking boat.

Silent days slip by,
quiet broken at times
as crabbed hands reach,

grab at something invisible,
confused words, terrors,
help me from parched lips.

Countenance again smoothes,
rough red skin now pink as a child's,
struggle and hurt sloughed off.

Above her pillowed head a painting—
broad river bends to hazy blue horizon,
a rowboat rests on near shore.

I wait with her for Charon
to take her across.

Quiet, Not Always Peaceful

1.

No sound escapes him as he kneels beside the bed,
reaches in palpable despair to embrace her, his wife,
his love, skeletal, in her last hours of breath.
Love speaks in sacred silence.

2.

Candle lit, gong struck, she sits,
eyes closed. Calm breaths,
outer mind releases.
Home.

3.

Traveling highway miles in silence,
state of grace: comfort shared
by two souls who know each other
well, need not speak.

4.

Orange and white koi swim slowly
in round, patient patterns.
Moss and ferns grow along the rocks
where she sits.

Her Dystopian Vision

My voice is mute,
   sadness pulls at my throat,
     eclipses sound.

Barren fields,
   empty forests
      waterways fouled,
   oceans, lifeless.

Great cities
   submerged,
     disease
       rife,
   civilization
under siege.

I turn,
   search
     bleak
sky.

Ghost birds fly,
     invisible,
  silent.

Even a Goddess Despairs

Raven-haired beauty of ancient Greece, goddess revered, worshipped for fertility and flowers and joy of all growing greenness, Persephone today is overcome with grief.

Earth, her bountiful Garden, burns, floods, melts, becomes desert. More quickly than Icarus, birds plummet from poisoned skies. Glorious creatures—Tigers, Giraffes, Butterflies, Frogs, Elephants— disappear, forever silenced.

A Dialectic Tale for Our Time

I heard
   the jays screaming blue,
      the sky was black, seething
                with roiling clouds,
     dark birds curving the air,
       churning   in winds of fear.

The ground ripped   & split,
      pulled   apart.   Birches eyed
         their dividing world
    open-   mouthed,
white branches shaking
              against the somber sky
  in   disjointed   frenzy,
    earth's body convulsing
in yaws,   cracks,   & caverns.

I saw
   the ancients come,
      harvest   what had been.
     The Quiet Voice said
        Let it go;
      tears   deluged my face.

Light sparked
     a sea
       of stars
         spinning,
           holding the sky
      in waves
  of glowing pulsation.

The sun returned.
    Spiders emerged,   began to spin,
       recreate the story,   the world,
    reorder   time & space.

The birches steadied, wren sang.
    Turtle again walked the dappled wood.

Temple of the Goddess
A Litany for Persephone

The temple of love
temple of light
temple of darkness
and of flight
of wonder and of awe
of dybbuks, the devil, flaw
of pure and pollution
the divine and diminution
temple of feasts and celebration
of failure, contamination
of fast and furious,
slow and spurious
laughter, pain
the absurd, insane
of water, air, evil, despair
of joy, birth, and expansion
bitterness, loss, contraction
of body, of earth
spirit, mirth
of fire, soul, and
all made Whole.

Persephone did not come with me to Florida,

she was there already, nurturing the profusion of palms and blooming white frangipani, gardenia, and pink bougainvillea, delighting in sunshine and cerulean skies.

But I wonder, can she ignore the endless plethora of highways and shopping malls? Do they lower her spirits as they do mine?

We walked the path by the Intracoastal together—smooth grey driftwood along sandy banks, stoic pelicans flying the drawbridge, a pair of mourning doves frightened into flight, their sound sweet and squeaky-strange, like The Three Stooges' *wooo-woo-woo-wa-wooo*.

I savored meals of luscious grouper, crab and scallop in the camaraderie of husband and friends, reveled in moments of a son's companionship, danced with abandon at a glamorous dinner club. No glimpse of Persephone there!

Did she return before me to the wintery Northeast, buried in the underground of coats, hats, scarves and gloves, boots, warm socks? Did she watch Punxsutawney Phil on TV to hear there were six more weeks until spring? And did she care a jot about the Super Bowl and bawdy halftime show?

Back home I find myself cranky, disoriented, overwhelmed—by gobs of laundry, incessantly grey skies, stinging icy air, piles of mail, dark, heavy clothing, daily wretched news that hits the gut like a calving glacier, and the inevitable failure to accomplish all that needs doing.

My pay-back for going away. The price of being human. And mortal.

Special Acknowledgments

With deepest gratitude I thank Gladys Henderson for her generous encouragement and skillful review and shaping of my manuscript. Her assistance, guidance, and friendship brought the brightest light to those days.

Many thanks to the talented, accomplished women of Poets Circle who have taught me so much over the years about poetry and life—Sybil Bank, Sasha Ettinger, Evelyn Kandel, Rita Katz, and Rosemary Walsh. Their helpful reviews and support of early versions of these poems were immeasurably beneficial. With additional appreciation to Rosemary Walsh for her extra time and assistance in editing earlier versions of many of these poems.

And to Victoria Camp I offer thanks for her friendship and selfless help in creating beautiful promotional materials for this book.

Thank you to Sherri Deutsch at Deutsch Photography for her editing.

I must acknowledge the work of Dr. Jean Shinoda Bolen, Jungian analyst, feminist, author, and online workshop presenter. Her informing books *Goddesses in Everywoman* and *Goddesses in Older Women* and workshop helped inspire and unleash my archetypal relationship with the great Greek goddess, Persephone.

With thanks always (eternally!) to my loving, patient, and supportive husband, Michael Sears.

www.ingramcontent.com/pod-product-compliance
Lightning Source LLC
LaVergne TN
LVHW041558070426
835507LV00011B/1161